Me and My Pia

Repertoire *for the young pianist*

Composed and edited by Fanny Waterman

Dear Young Pianist

The pieces in this beautifully-illustrated collection have been specially composed and arranged to help you to enjoy learning the piano. Have you ever watched a spider waltz, been to Hong Kong during the rush hour, attended a huntsman's funeral, or watched a royal procession? You will find all these pieces and many more in **Me and My Piano Repertoire**.

Have fun, and practise every day!

Fanny Waterman.

FABER *ff* MUSIC

Contents

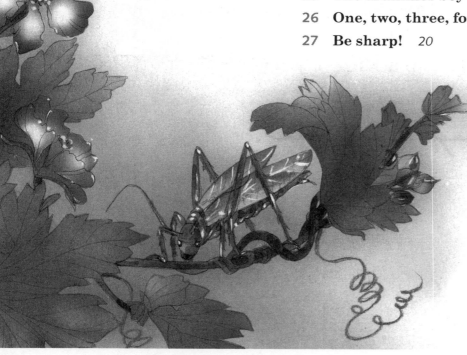

First published in 1992 by Faber Music Ltd
This edition © 2008 by Faber Music Ltd
Bloomsbury House 74–77 Great Russell Street London WC1B 3DA
Music setting by Jeanne Roberts
Illustrated by Julia Osorno
Cover design by Lydia Merrills-Ashcroft
Page design by Susan Clarke
Printed in England by Caligraving Ltd
All rights reserved

ISBN10: 0-571-53202-0
EAN13: 978-0-571-53202-5

1 School march

2 Winter frost

3 Two old gypsies

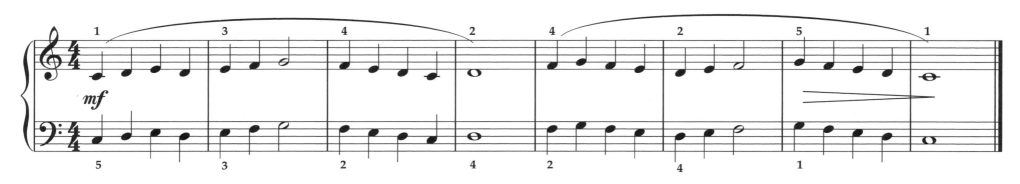

4 On the swing

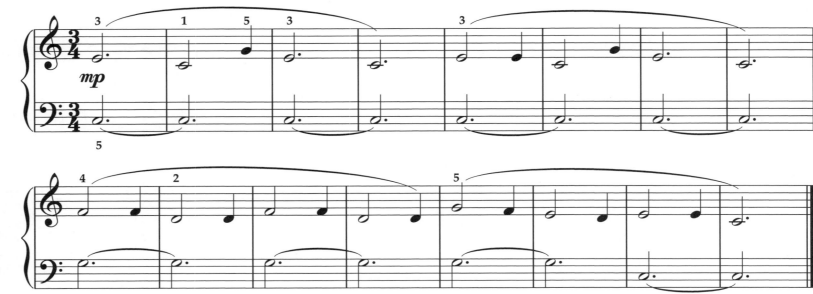

5 Folk song

6 Hopping frog

7 Follow my leader

8 Cossack dance

9 Pony trot

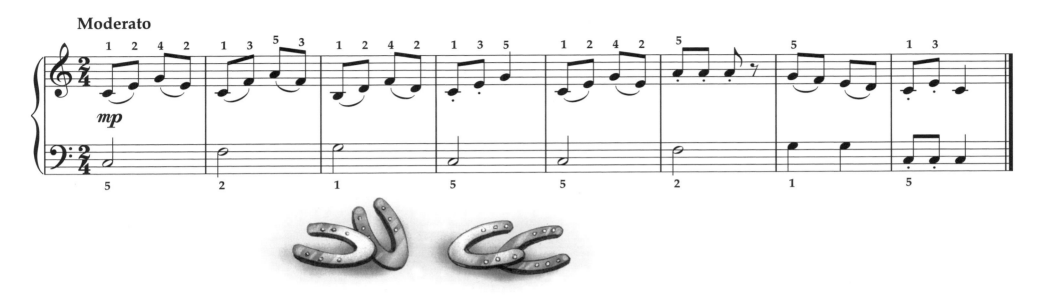

10 Up and down

11 Spider's waltz

12 The skipping game

13 Moonlight

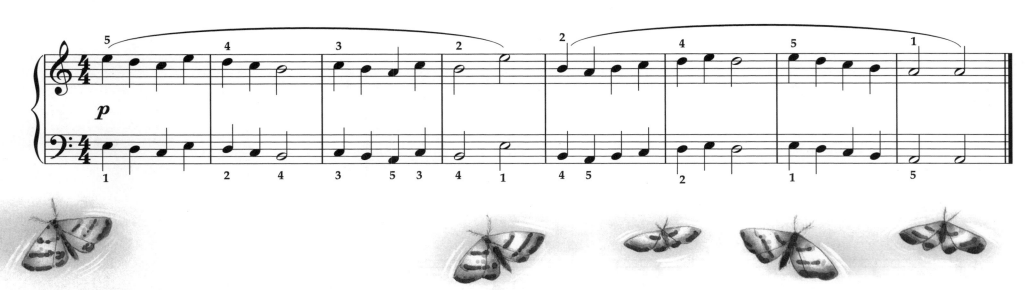

14 Tick tock

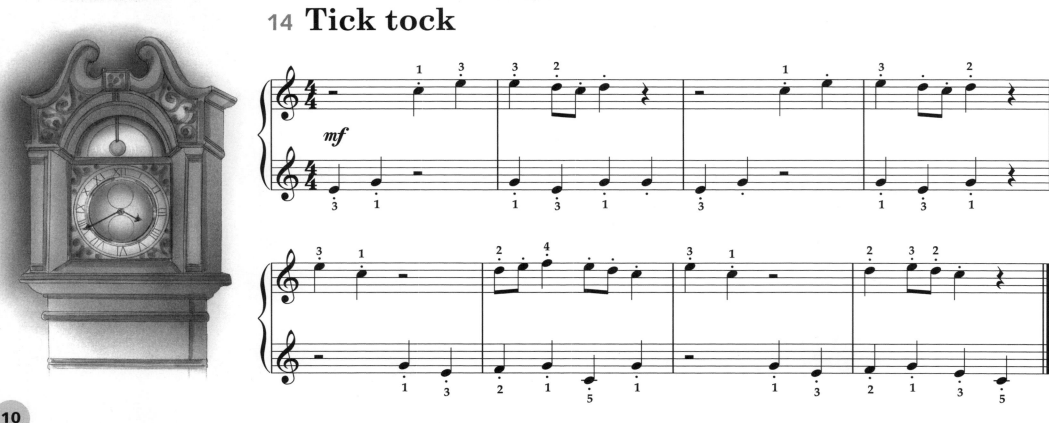

15 Playing together

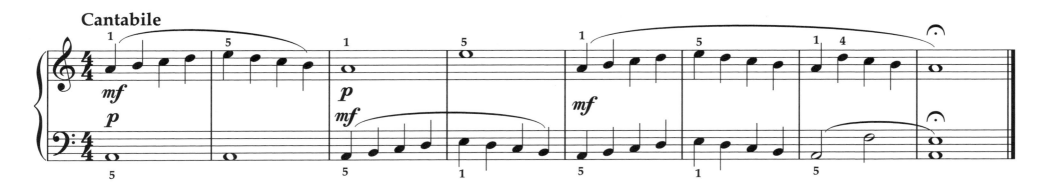

Cantabile

16 Pop goes the weasel

POP!

17 Mountain song

18 Sailors' dance

19 The sun has got his hat on

20 Suo-gân (Welsh lullaby)

21 Winter is here! (German folk song)

22 The cello's tune

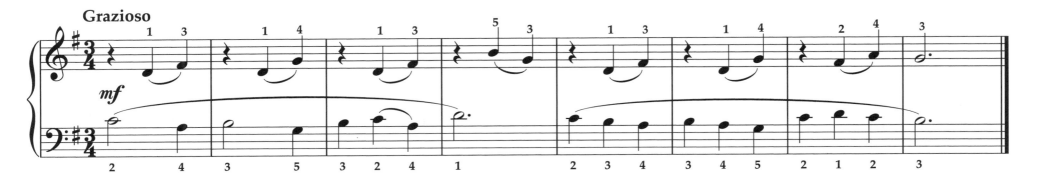

23 **Daisy, Daisy** (duet)   Secondo

23 **Daisy, Daisy** (duet) Primo

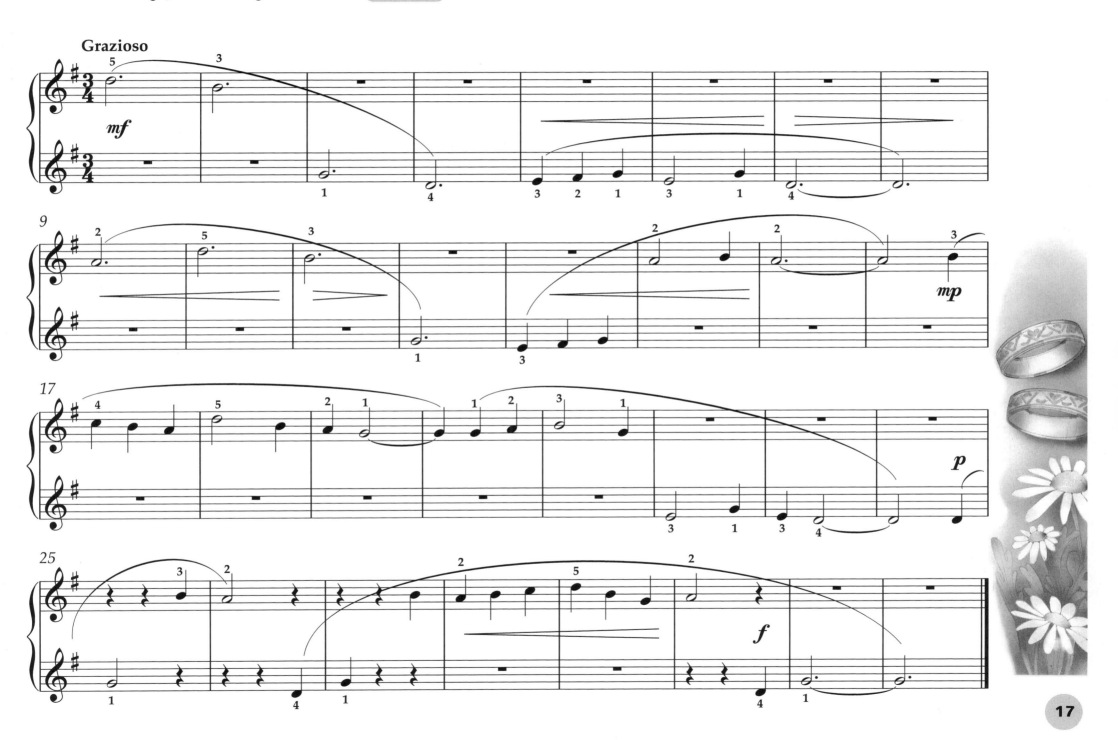

24 Royal procession

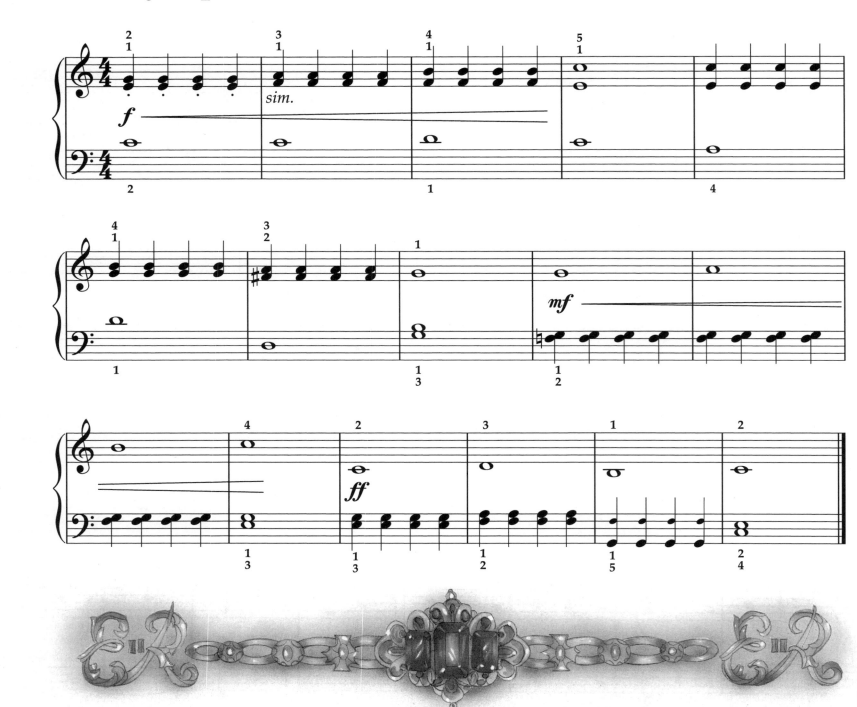

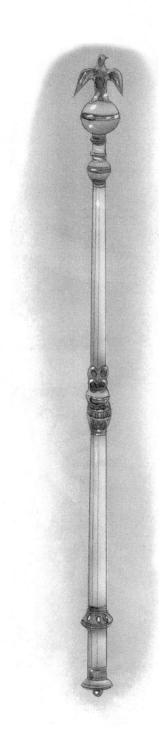

25 The drummer boy

Tempo di Marcia

Go on playing chords in the left hand for as long as you want, making a gradual *diminuendo*.

26 One, two, three, four, five

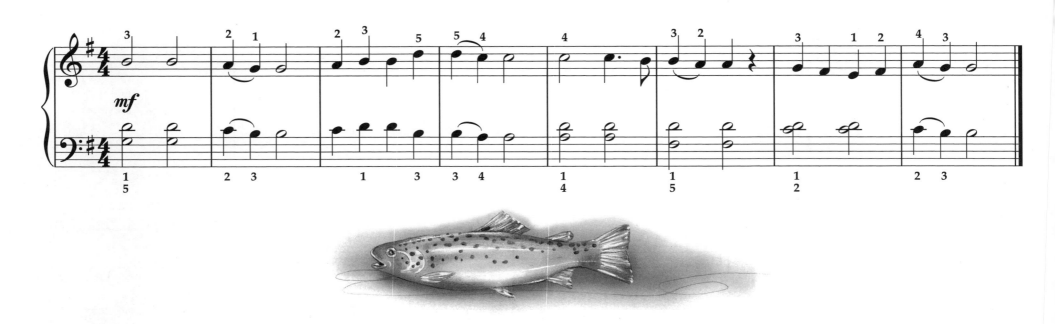

27 Be sharp!

28 Little Bo-Peep

29 Decorating the Christmas tree

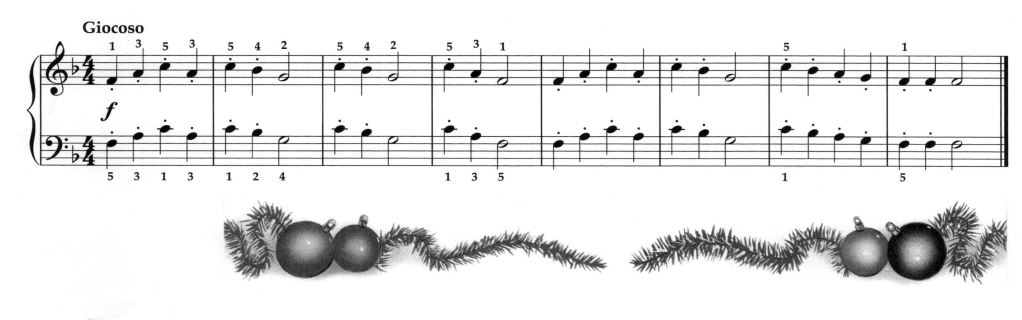

30 Hot cross buns

31 The fly and the bumblebee

32 The rainbow

Put both pedals down all the way through if you can reach them.

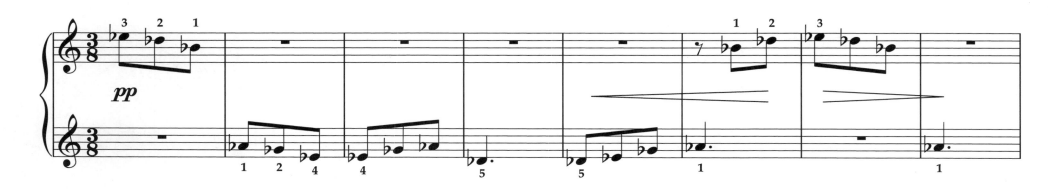

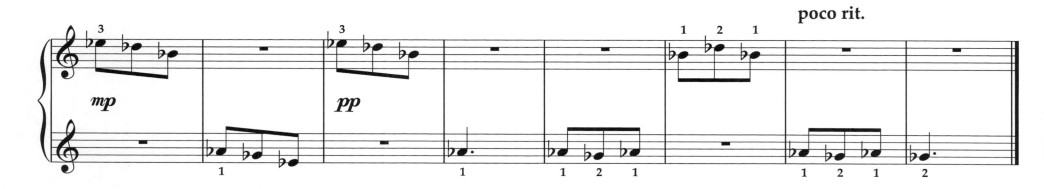

33 Rush hour in Hong Kong

Continue playing D♭ with your left hand.

34 The little birch tree

35 The huntsman's funeral

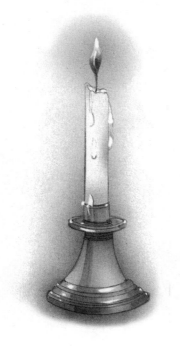

36 Study

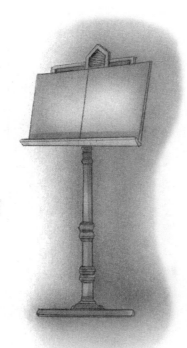

37 Dame, get up and bake your pies

38 Home sweet home

39 Early one morning

40 Raindrops

41 Praise Him, praise Him

42 Hatikvah (Israeli national anthem)

43 Here's a health unto her Majesty

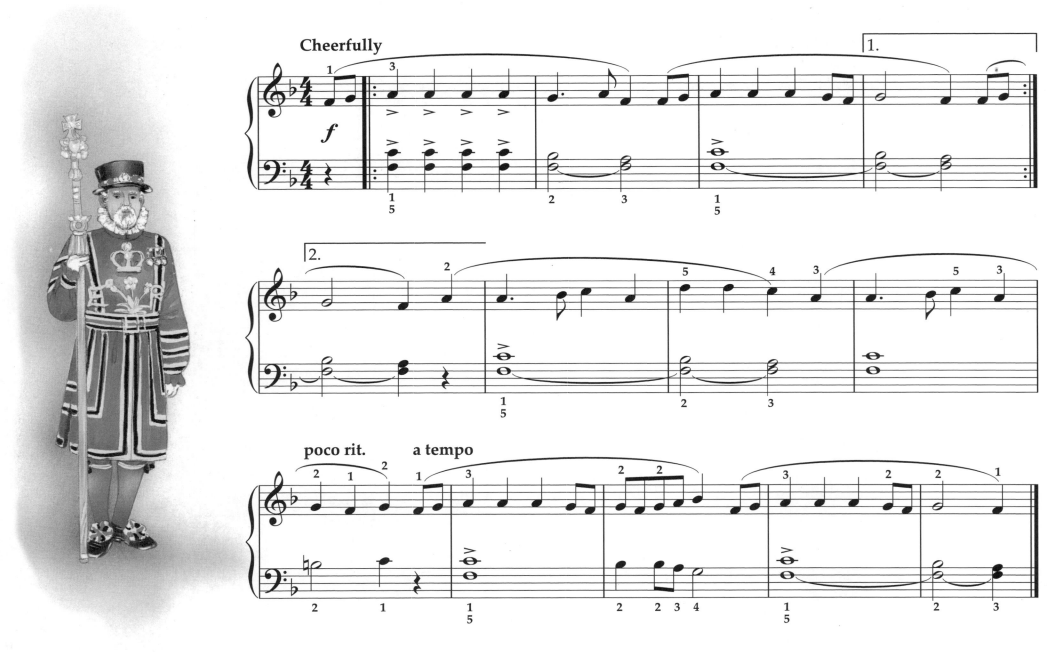